GROWING UP
IN THE 60s

September 1960. Australian Mythic! Eve and Geoff Thompson,
Graham and Lesley (from left), Helen and Sue on the table,
Tom contemplates the flag.

GROWING UP
IN THE 60s

TOM THOMPSON
WITH SOME DRAWINGS
BY MARTIN SHARP

ETT IMPRINT
EXILE BAY

ACKNOWLEDGEMENTS

This book was originally written for Simon Marnie who produced our 'Electric Bookwatch' program on 2JJJ. The author would like to thank the following people for their input into the writing of this book - Elizabeth Butel, Bronwyn Kemp, Kim Benjamin, Wendy Walsh and Martin Sharp; and with its revival as an ABC Radio serial in 2013 - Gary Norwell and Allan vander Linden (King Biscuit), Reg Mombassa and Peter O'Doherty (Dog Trumpet) and Suzanne Hill at ABC's 'Night Life'.

This edition published in 2020 by ETT Imprint, Exile Bay

First published in 1986 by Kangaroo Press, Kenthurst
Extended version with music first broadcast by ABC Radio in 2013
First audio edition by Bolinda Audio 2013
First electronic edition ETT Imprint 2020

ISBN 978-0-6487390-1-2 (ebk)
ISBN 978-0-6487390-2-9 (pbk)

Cover by Tim Martin
Designed by Eliothe Ruthgarde

CONTENTS

Following the full effects of the fireball, I was now 'ready to go!'

My sister Lesley, gaily driving our '1936 Studebaker', Parkes 1953.

PRELUDE

In 1953, fireballs raced through the valleys around Parkes, New South Wales.

Things looked grim from where I was. I was contemplating a navel and it wasn't mine!

My father had built a ute out of twenty different vehicles. It was dubbed a 1936 Studebaker, because of its radiator. Dad then built a garage for it and was finishing the first steel-framed house in town, on a little spread of apricot and almond trees. It was seven years before the Sixties would begin and the radio telescope was opening up to the heavens and welcoming things from other planets, drawing energy back to Parkes, our home town.

Three weeks before I was born, a fireball flew into the house. The front and back doors were open, and my mother and of course, *moi*, were sitting on the lounge resting from the heat… She must have sensed a knocking at the open door, got up to look, and a fireball as big as a beach ball flew past us at belly height – and shot through the front door into the valleys of Parkes.

My father duly noted in his diary:
Fireball goes through house
Eve goes to hospital
Must shut back door…

When I was born at Rosedurnate hospital my mother told the doctor:
'I have seen the future Doctor and it is all paisley and flares! There are flowers everywhere… Doctor… and all the boys have incredibly long hair!'

In my cot by her bedside, my little ears pricked up.

FREEDOM

In 1960 my family lived in a large country town in New South Wales. My parents talked of owning a house, my teenage brother of owning a car, my sister of extending her education. As the middle child, seven years old, I was confident too. I dreamt of staying out late at night.

We lived in a three-bedroomed brick house near the town centre. In 1960, before the satellite towns, the end of our street was the edge of town. The rest was paddock, slowly being pegged out by families wanting homes of their own.

Next door to us was a newsagency where I swapped Mad magazines to give to my brother who spent a lot of time lying about the house. He was seventeen, wore a black woollen coat (even in summer), wouldn't ever weed the garden and was a hero fit for me. My brother's bedroom was an Aladdin's cave of cheap electrics. He had a Hornby Dubblo railway set, moving Meccano, a ham radio, a tape recorder which couldn't record music and a record player, just for singles.

My brother played rebel music in his bedroom next to mine, like *Summertime Blues* by Eddie Cochran, when he should have been playing *Lonely Boy* by clean-cut Paul Anka. When he'd go next door to watch *Six O'Clock Rock* on the neighbour's television, I'd go in his room and play Johnny O'Keefe or Sheb Woolley's *Purple People Eater*. I longed to be bold enough to paint ELVIS IS KING in twelve-foot high like him, red letters on my school quadrangle, but then, that was teenage business. Kids like me were still struggling with Dr Spock.

How was I to know that my parent's addiction to the theories of Dr Spock (the Baby's Friend) would mean freedom... It was late one January night and I was walking back from a friend's house at the end of our street. A full moon was up, and I tiptoed along the steel-railed animal pens of the stock- yards. When I stopped in the middle, six feet above the ground, feeling the fence sway to the movements of the cattle somewhere in the blackness below, I realised it was not just late, it was incredibly late. The latest I'd been out, and that I was not afraid of being out in the dark or away from home. The pleasure of being by myself in the night was 'home' in itself, and this pleasure continued for the mile walk back down Trail Street, Wagga Wagga.

Elvis in Parkes! Well not quite but my brother was right, well before the Elvis Festival in Parkes. Australia received the Elvis Comeback *TV special 24 hours before the USA; so Elvis played Parkes first!*

Dad with his WW2 medals, Lesley, Helen, Tom and Sue.

ANZAC DAY 1960

My brother took this photo of our family at the back of our house under the grapevines. My father had just returned from the annual Anzac Day march and for the only time in his life he'd worn his medals. I was very proud of his medals but my father was not so sure about them, and talked very quietly about the war. He made me think it was not the great adventure it had been cracked up to be.

This was also the same day my brother received a letter on the back of a postage stamp. It was from his friend Warren down the road, and was addressed to Comrade Nikiti Thomski. In those Cold War days the postman came twice daily, and he'd dutifully delivered it. It had not been opened by any secret agents. Penetrating the patriotic defences of Wagga Wagga was probably too much of a challenge for the KGB.

At school I had just survived my first leading role in a class play, as one of the shepherds observing a late Christmas drama. My arrival on the scene was greeted with waves of laughter, as I clutched my woolly lamb by the tail, holding it away from my body, looking saintly. Realising the source of all this mirth, I dropped the lamb onto a startled lap, and exited.

My father, realising the possibility of a great theatrical career was in sight, took me to see a local production of Gilbert & Sullivan's *The Pirates of Penzance*—at night! I sat spellbound by the colour, waiting for an explanation or a mention of the mysterious Dr Spock. Nothing was forthcoming but I came out of that theatre realising that there was more to music than rock-and-roll; for one thing there were jokes.

I cracked my first joke in October 1960. My brother was talking about Kruschev while reading the papers in bed. With all the subtlety of my seven years I made a joke about the word 'Kruschev'. I knew that it was a success because my brother laughed. So I repeated it. He then told me not to repeat a joke at which I promptly forgot the joke for all time, not yet realising the great truth that lies behind all good jokes. You can repeat them ad infinitum, but not to the same person. However, I had at last made a joke and one with topical content. Did this mean I was political?

Kruschev slams his shoe down at the United Nations,
not quite Blue Suede, but 'Nyet', that would do
when there are no Russian Rockers on the air waves.

SMOKE DREAMS OF YOU

Smoking was a vice I was told. This made it sound appealing. At the end of 1960, still with the sounds of *Tom Dooley*, *Bird Dog* and *The Purple People Eater* chugging away in my brain, I made good use of the threepences my brother had collected over the years, which lay hidden along the top of his wardrobe. I used them to win packets of cigarettes at the local show. The road to dissipation was simple. All you had to do was throw a threepence on one of the packets of cigarettes that were lined up in neat rows across a table. If it landed squarely on the packet, then it was yours. My years of hoopla training stood me in good stead. I won twenty packets, much to the chagrin of the spotty youths with greasy hair whose girlfriends lounged behind in silent condemnation. As my father drove us home I was elated, twenty packets of Craven A and Turf stuffed inside my clothes. It was then I made the decision. Honour demanded I should smoke them all.

Someone had to teach me, however, and in great secrecy. The enigmatic Spock had allowed me some freedoms but smoking, from what my parents gave me to understand, was definitely not one of them. Margaret, my thirteen-year-old neighbour, was more understanding. We met in the vacant allotment behind both our homes (the one I'd almost burnt to the ground two years before when I belatedly discovered matchsticks) and proceeded to indulge in my first vice.

At church I'd been told that 'Vice is always followed by more Vice', but at that tender age I could not think of a more suitable follow-up. I chose the packet of Craven A because it had a pretty, whiskered cat on the front. I liked cats. We both sat hunched in our shorts behind the trees, hoping that no one would see the smoke. But when I drew back, disaster—I coughed my lungs out. I liked the taste, I liked Margaret and I liked the cat but from then on smoking was not for me. I gave Margaret the twenty packets and looked for other vices, but that is another story.

Quality and Purity.. Well I ain't
superstitious but a Black Cat crossed
my... well everything from the neck
down.

THE ITINERANT LIFE

All my friends seemed to live in hotels. Their parents were all building their own home on a block of land just out of town and were living very cheaply above the shiny steel kegs, local drunks and sweet smells of warm beer. These urchins were all aching to steal my brother's scale model steam-engine, which I had inherited, and when they succeeded I tramped the bars and corridors of each hotel, looking for the likely offender. It was a strange sensation to see so many people living in such close quarters under the same roof. Like a holiday camp, or life aboard an ocean liner, an existence for which I secretly longed. My investigations were to no avail. The thief had probably boiled down the parts on the hotel stove and was busy constructing new and complex machinery.

Armed with the latest *Mad* magazine and Alfred E. Neuman's motto: 'What? Me worry!', I forgot to tell my brother about the tragedy for the next decade. Luckily he was by now more interested in cars than steam engines. Cars and girls. . . My idea of a car was one like our 1938 Dodge — wide enough for me to lie down on the floor of the back seat, massaged by everybody else's feet. During the winter, which was really cold in Wagga, I could feel the warmth of the chassis and the road below, and fall asleep to the dull roar of the engine, sucking on a Marella Jube.

We travelled all the time because my father worked for the Department of Main Roads. Judging by the places we travelled it was clearly his ambition to sample every minor and major road in the state. Travel was a substitute for television, a luxury we did not possess. We travelled far and wide—even to Canberra! The event is commemorated in a photograph taken at my grandmother's in Sydney, in which I am holding a flag as a memento of my first trip to the corridors of power, the dioramas at the War Memorial and the metal cigarette case which was pierced by a bullet thus saving its owner's life. So much for the evils of smoking I reflected.

Every time we went to Sydney we saw all our family, who in numbers could have formed a vigorous platoon. We always stayed at my grand-mother's and looked in on my only living grandfather. After these visits we returned to Wagga via Lithgow, Cowra and Young. Once, just west of Cowra, at 10 p.m. we saw a rainbow by moonlight. I slid back on the leather seat. Was this a sign? Perhaps it was for this was to be the last time the whole family travelled to Sydney together and the decade was only just beginning.

SUMMER HOLIDAYS

Under immense pressure from my brother, my father was persuaded to buy a new car. When he arrived home in a 1948 Chevrolet my brother was not amused. I said, "A *new* car Dad!" The welder next door had made a trailer for all the camping equipment our family required on our annual holidays—tents, ropes and toys.

We would always pitch a tent just above the beach at Durras, on the far south coast of New South Wales, no matter where we may have moved in the intervening year. My father had been camping at Durras since 1933, when he was a boy, and Durras continued to be the meeting place for our extended family. While some of our cousins might rent a flat nearby, most would set up their tents near ours in a family cluster.

Our holidays would always last at least a month, although time became elastic thanks to the family rituals of camping, fishing, swimming, sleeping and eating. Camping was the single word for putting up and maintaining the tent against the elements. Putting up the tent was usually accomplished in the headlights of our Chevrolet with the occasional curse from my father if the wind was high or it was raining. I would place the tent pegs and beat them into the ground with a hammer, while my father jostled with the tent, aided by my elder brother. My mother would be creating a meal in the boot of the car. My elder sister would take care of the young ones, binding them up with laughter on the back seat.

Once the tent was up, and the mosquito nets down, the Tilley lamps would be set, stretchers and bedding laid out, the Primus lit and the evening meal would arrive, with glistening cutlery on the makeshift table. After the first night, the daily fare inevitably would be fish.

Fishing was a skill that was passed down from father to son in our family. My grandfather Joe was a notable rock fisherman who could fling a sixteen- foot rod and line way out to sea with great success. Groper, snapper and flathead leapt at his every bait. . . He taught my father well, and my father spent long hours with me by the curling waves, teaching me how to rig a line, select the right hook, spear crabs, carve cunjevoi from the rocks for bait, and cast a line beyond a jutting reef.

We'd often spend a day together at Flat Rock, talking quietly on the rock platform in the heat, watching the swell with one eye out for 'the big wave' which just might swamp us. The fish below, nibbling away at our bait... I'd soon be dreaming away about what sort of fish I'd catch when I grew up, just idling along with the waves on the horizon.

Swimming was ritual number three. Everyday. All my cousins were great swimmers, having been born near a Johnston outboard motor. But not me. 'Dust on my lungs' I'd say, pointing west. Any excuse! I loved the water but hated the surf, and became king of the rock pools, chasing the gulls along the beach or building complex waterways for castles in the sand. I'd build them up frantically at high tide, hoping they might survive their nightly battering, with no luck.

Back up on the dunes, us kids would play chasings while the adults set the next ritual into motion: eating. The lights dancing in the marquees at dusk and the smell of fish, or simple fare. Home-cooked meals; fish and chips, or baked potatoes, steamed vegetables, lamb chops with mustard sauce, peas and beans, mashed potato and something orange: steamed carrots or baked pumpkin. 'Scrumptious!' I also liked eating 'trees' (broccoli) because they were a test to eat delicately, any curry and a special dish—'toad-in-the-hole'—meat cooked in a pastry.

After tea, my younger sisters would play with cut-out Barbie dolls while the rest of the family would play Scrabble on a card table, thanks to

My first fish - a rock cod - taken at Flat Rock, Durras, while humming to Fabian's String Along.

a Hurricane lamp. My mother usually won, having the uncanny ability to produce a seven-letter word on a triple word score just before the end of the game. I lost, sulking for years.

Sleeping in a tent by the sea was so comforting. We never thought of intruders, and never had them. My mother would make up little beds on the stretchers and we could read by the light of a lamp. My younger sisters read Enid Blyton and I read comics with names like *Commando* and *Battleground*. In my dreams, characters said 'Eat lead!' and 'Achtung!'. My parents would spend the evening with one of my father's family, drinking tea with homemade biscuits at one end of the tent. We'd fall asleep to the sound of the sea, dreaming of cardboard dolls or flying fish, the perfect beach and the days strung out ahead of us.

A seven letter word for Scrabble deemed unacceptable by my mother.

SYDNEY... THE BIG SMOKE

In 1961 we had to move from our country town to Sydney, and live in the suburb of Beverly Hills. The name of our suburb forced my parents to buy a Pye TV so we could observe our prototypes in *The Beverly Hillbillies*. Culturally deprived no longer, at least we could join the real world of advertising and current events. Like Elly May and the rest of the Hillbilly clan we were wide-eyed at the commercials—'Louie the fly', 'the Flick man', and the hauntingly logical 'Use a Roller Door . . . That's what it's for!'

My elder brother and sister were particularly happy as they were old enough to stay up and see programs about vice. Like *Seventy Seven Sunset Strip* (barp, barp), *Bonanza* (dumdiddledum dumdiddledum dumdiddledumdah dah) and *The Untouchables* (barm barm barm!).

I was allowed to collect stamps, so I specialised in Nude Majas and other 'Art' works, scouring the arcades of Sydney for major paintings with perforations. Among the magic shops, second-hand bookshops and other more specialist lines I would spend my shillings like a miser, keeping my patient mother waiting, reading the *Woman's Day*.

My father, a natural historian, was very concerned that great events were passing us by. On the day that the last tram ran in Sydney he took me for a final ride. It was 25 February and we crammed into Tram no. 1995 in Elizabeth Street to go a few blocks into history. The next morn-ning they were gone. No more gleaming blinds or magical journeys at dusk on a summer's evening, fresh breezes blowing through the wide open doors. No more unscrupulous men with newspapers threatening exposure to genteel ladies sitting opposite. No more conductors hanging off the side of crowded trams and collecting fares from the perilous ledge on the outside. Lying awake while the older ones watched *Consider Your Verdict*, I watched the strings of trams shunt out and into the ethereal world, leaving only the smell of dieseline buses.

By now my brother was totally car crazy, particularly over small cars like the latest racing Mini Coopers. I liked them because they were my size: baby cars. I was on the spot to watch him buy his first car, a 1953 Singer. My mother had said yes, thinking she was getting a sewing machine. We towed it home where it proceeded to rot in the front yard. The Singer would never be fast enough for my brother.

By now he was also at University. Well, that's what he told me. I knew he spent most of his time reading papers in bed and listening to the Dell-tones. He was studying to be an engineer. I thought he was studying to be a delinquent.

I, however, was an honourable child. I started a Detective Club and promptly found a dog's collar. Alas, I received no reward and failed to locate the lucky dog. I decided to be more like *Robert Taylor's Detectives*, which I was now allowed to watch for fifteen minutes before the vice set in. Observing their hulk and bulk in comparison to my own bird-like frame I wrote off to Charles Atlas. Charles Atlas could not have realised I was a skinny eight-year-old and wanted to charge me twenty-five pounds for his Strength Course. I salted his many lesser requests away amongst the stamps. It wasn't until he demanded only one pound that I seriously looked at myself in the mirror. Realising that I had only a few shillings in the bank I drew a veil across my aspirations to herculean girth, wore three sets of clothing and began jujitsu, a free interpretation of the ancient oriental art, which I performed in pyjamas in my bedroom. With these ploys I talked myself out of many a school fight.

On my eighth birthday, armed with a black belt, I was taken into the city by my father for a day of indulgence. Perhaps he'd had a letter from Dr Spock? We saw *How the West was Won* in Cinemascope, an experience that resembled all I had read about seasickness, as successive waves

Helping my brother Graham support a road sign on the Brown Mountain, near Bega, that had been dealt with in the great Australian manner - using a 303 rifle!

of horse and wagon crushed us into our seats. He also took me to Luna Park and afterwards we walked back across the Harbour Bridge. Sydney Harbour, what a place! The ferries seemed as big as passenger liners and glowed in the dark when we had to go home. Those neon lights were glowing even when we'd got home, blinking out 'adventure'.

It was almost the end of the year when my brother finally got the car he always wanted—a lovely 'red sloper' Jowett Javelin. He even got a second one for parts and proceeded to demolish it with much cheering from myself. It was only after he'd completely obliterated it that we realised he'd smashed up the customised one. Christmas was to be pretty bleak that year.

Graham with his Jowett Javelin, and Helen, both clearly keener on this than our 1948 Chevrolet.

SPIKE MILLIGAN OFFERS
AUSTRALIA HOPE

Spike Milligan arrived in Australia in July 1962.   I loved listening to his craziness on *The Goon Show* over ABC radio. He was talking about his new Australian series and as usual he had that mad, faraway cackle in his voice:

The new radio show? Well one deals with Australia's entry into the America's Cup yacht race. . . First we have a very patriotic Australian builder who constructs the challenger by knitting a yacht out of wool. When the Americans see the woolly yacht— highlighting one of Australia's major exports— they decide it's time for them to build a yacht to show off their main product. So they build a yacht out of compressed divorce petitions and melted down Elvis Presley records—using the disc hole to place the masts.

Ben Lexcen and I were both listening in.

WITH THE PHANTOM
IN DARKEST AFRICA

In 1962 I had every phantom ring that could be bought. My knuckles shone in the dark with jewels from darkest Africa. I ran through the paspalum in the park on the lookout for deadly Pygmies, or pirates on the seven swings. Things were perfect, except that I lived in a three-bedroomed, brick-veneer house instead of a cave, and we were a three-car family, when you counted the crushed Javelin. I was allowed up to see *The Rifleman* (blam blam blam) and realised that the city was more dangerous than living in the country and that's why I wasn't allowed out as much. However, I was allowed in for longer periods.

There were lots of ballads on the radio, like Gene Pitney's *Only Love Can Break a Heart*, but I was more interested in *Duke of Earl*, *Esso Besso* (although I wondered what petrol could possibly have to do with kissing) and *The Monster Mash*. My brother had left University for a job, no doubt so he could add things to his car. He was racing with a local club and winning trophies. When, I wondered, would real life begin for me? I longed for a trophy but got instead a pair of white mice. At last, a chance to be responsible! I realised that I was not yet ready for manhood when one escaped and was eaten by Nelson, the one-eyed cat from next door. The other suffocated shortly after when its wire-fronted cage fell onto the laundry floor. Stung by this double tragedy I was glad to hear that we were leaving the city and going back to the country to live. There I could roam free, commune with nature and build up my muscles by beating back the bush.

I burned Charles Atlas's letters in anticipation.

Phantom # 196, 1961 was first published in the
Australian Woman's Mirror in 1938, showing once
again that the Phantom was - timeless.,

DR SPOCK AND
SPUTNIK 1

It all happened at once. My voice broke and the twelve year old bully at the top of my street decided to wrestle me into oblivion every afternoon. Walking home from school, he'd say, 'So you think you're a grown-up now with gravel in your voice. Take that!" And he held my throat in an Indian Death-Lock.

'Why don't you fight me?' he'd say.

'I don't want to hurt you,' I'd say quietly, as he strangled me.

'You've got to fight me!' he'd say, heating up.

'I don't want to use... my - my (what was that term I read once)... my Kung Fu-'

He immediately released his ferocious grip: 'But next time Gravel-voice, you've got to use your Fu – or I will bash you!'

Oh, what a poet! And what a relief it was to get home and find out we were leaving town, real soon; the family splitting up and the unmasking of that shadowy figure who had dogged my footsteps since birth—Dr Spock.

I'd just got back from seeing my friend John Grierson when it happened. John's father had given me ten shillings as a parting gift, a fortune in sweets, and had explained to all of us why my voice was deeper than John's on the tape recorder—how it had . . . broken...

I thought for a moment that the local bully must have done that with his Chief Little Wolf Death hold, but it seems that I was just growing up and all these changes were part of it.

Clutching my first ten shilling note I had asked him 'Does Dr Spock have anything to do with this?' And he did. Dr Spock, I was informed, was an American doctor who advocated freedom for babies, no strict rules. I was a Spock baby, or so my parents said. I thanked him in my deepest voice, waved goodbye and walked home thinking what the Russians might be doing to their babies right now. Was there a Russian Dr Spockski? If so then their babies were probably all linked up to Sputnik 1.

On the way home from John's I was again attacked by the local bully. After much calm grunting on my part, I finally could say, 'I will show you all my Kung Fu holds on Saturday…'

He was pretty happy with that and let me go home, shaken but not stirred.

At home the family were clustered round a map of Australia, planning the trip to Broken Hill. I was told that this old gold town was 700 miles west of Sydney, in the desert, and that my brother and sister were staying on in Sydney, leaving just the five of us. So I was to become the eldest child!

'Does that mean I can watch more TV?' I asked, wishing to establish my rights early. And it did. What a comfort. As well, I was to accompany my father in the 1948 Chevrolet all the way to Broken Hill. It would take a biblical three days and three nights to get there, while my mother and two sisters would shuffle along in the Silver City Comet. It sounded like the kind of thing an eldest child must do. It sounded heroic.

And on Saturday when we were leaving town I saw the local bully mowing the lawn. I asked Dad to slow, right down, so I could wave goodbye to him for the last long time.

ON THE ROAD

All I remember about the first 2 00 m iles w ere t he l ollies d isappearing across the distance. There go the Red and Green Blocks, Licorice Straps, Slate Pencils, Musk, Snakes, Pretty Babies, Metro Gum and a fleet of Battleships and battalion of Aussie Hats. I suppose if I had been older I would have finally got through those twenty packets of cigarettes.

The miles I'd seen before on previous trips and it wasn't until we got to Cobar out in the western desert that I realised I was far away from home in an alien land. It was dry, brittle and very hot. Even at night. We found ourselves staying in a country hotel on the main street. A little nest of rooms with surgical white sheets and a balcony overlooking a strip of bitumen.

We walked in the evening, my father and I, down to the open-air cinema, hidden away behind sheets of corrugated iron. Squinting through the cracks I could see the locals, sitting out in deck chairs, drinking glasses of cool beer and rocking in time with the shutter-speed of the old projector. It was too late to join them so we went back to the hotel to bed.

Moving west, the road ahead of us was almost straight, the weather prickling with a dry heat. There was saltbush by the side of the road and the occasional emu. I sat with no lollies to whittle away the miles, frying on the leather seat.

When we arrived in Wilcannia it was like a town from the old West. Verandas were slung along the road. Aboriginals in cowboy boots sipped beer with hamburgers. Down by the Darling River the local Aboriginals were camped under tin and bark humpies. The lights of Sydney Harbour had completely receded from view.

We arrived late that evening in Broken Hill, which was huddled among the low-lying hills of the Barrier Mountain Range. We found the rest of the family waiting at the Palace Hotel, just around the corner from the biggest two-up school in town. The roar in the evening air was from the winners and the losers.

Next morning we realised Broken Hill would be different. It was a union town and they'd declared the local Woolworths 'black', picketing out the front and reminding fellow unionists of the solemn occasion. On the streets there was virtual mass nudity. Shorts and thongs and not much more. It was perpetually summer, it seemed. I finally rolled down my long woollen socks.

It was the country life for me.

LOVE LETTERS
IN THE SAND

Our new home was built in 1880 with walls two-feet thick, large, red lacquered verandas and a six- foot high stone wall. It was white with grapevines, and almonds, apricots and figs grew in the yard. The house overlooked the town and it was heaven. I'd sit up in the cypress tree in the front yard, listening to the boy next door practising the trumpet while rereading my first love letter.

I knew it was a love letter because it was from 'the girl I left behind' in Wagga Wagga. Kerrie was only nine years old but was obviously a writer too:

Dear Tom, Susan and Helen

It's hot down here and every day we go the baths. How is Susan and Helen.

Love Kerrie

I knew it was a love letter because I read it over and over again, knowing that parts of it were especially meant for me. For Ray Brown and the Whispers, it was only to be *Twenty Miles*; for me and Kerrie, 700 miles apart, it was the beginning of the end.

Almost the first thing I learnt at school was that I was more interested in music. While I had trouble with grammar, mathematics and science, I had no difficulty with the golden hits of rock-and-roll. While I couldn't actually sing in tune, I could remember every word and rhythm behind anything that had the words 'love' or 'dance' in it. It's not that I wasn't good at school—coming from the city meant my teachers expected brilliance—it's just that I was more interested in extra-curricular activities: art, music, theatre and girls. My idea of sport, for instance, was just watching it.

Our last moment of TV in 1963, an ever-smiling Donna Reed with Montgomery Clift; soon to be tuned out in the Barrier Ranges leaving drifts of endless snow...

THE LONELIEST
TV IN THE WORLD

In that first year everyone in our school trooped up the hill and along our gravel drive. In 1963 we had the only TV in Broken Hill. On those rare days when it clouded over we could almost see a picture. People would line up just to see the 'snow'. Our 'snowie' was the envy of every child who ever spontaneously wanted electronic equipment.

These would be the years to pine after a Malvern Star bicycle, belting around the lanes of Broken Hill on my scooter, knowing that only children in cots should be riding scooters. Till my wish could be fulfilled I made sure that all my closest friends did have bikes. This enabled me to pooh-pooh their machines, gallantly walk home and get dinked for miles. For I was not born in Broken Hill ... I was an outsider.

It was in 1963 that I had my first bout of rabid existentialism. I was ten years old and had just won a signed photograph of Ray Brown and the Whispers at our local record shop when I made a decision. I bought my first record. My hard-earned 6s 8d was exchanged for a slip of vinyl with little orange stars on it, made in Germany. *My Bonnie*, by Tony Sheridan and the Beatles. The existential part was the words: '*My Bonnie lies over the ocean*'. All around me was desert. Futhermore I had never been overseas.

From then on my moods were almost instantly recognisable to others, including my family, by the chartbusters. All the essentials of learning

Martin Sharp's collage of the Beatles.

were to be found in the Beatles and the Supremes. Even the Dave Clark Five had something to teach me. The school of hard knocks became the school of Hard Rocks.

My best friend over the road settled it once and for all by his own anarchic gesture to the swinging sixties. Peter was a great Rolling Stones fan and could afford to buy their every disc. Having procured their latest single we would listen to the last cut in his lounge then each sit up one end of the room (having moved all the furniture to the sides). The ritual was his own invention—destroying the last Stones single to make way for the new. We'd whizz the plastic along the carpet from end to end until it broke up like a mirror ball. "*It's All Over Now*," Peter would say, philosophically. Even in Broken Hill we knew you had to live as if there were no tomorrow.

Peter was very good at sport. Every sport. Unlike me. Peter was in every team, whereas I avoided all of mine. Mysterious illnesses often struck me down. My in-built sense of aesthetics also had something to do with it. A clinching moment, proving that sport was not for me, was seeing our greatest sportsman, Evangeline Farros, at the Dareton interschool games. He was in his whites, and obviously sans underpants. It was more Michelangelo than Michael Jordon. A classic pose.

I did, however, like running. Particularly running to the lolly shop. Like any other ten-year-old who wanted to stay out late at night I found The Explorers Club. This was part of the church, sort of like a Wednesday night school for boys who might otherwise run away from home. At the Club there were a lot of minor sport activities for the inexpert like myself. And there were chalk chases at night and running round the block. These were the highlight of my week. Running flat out with a piece of chalk, trying to befuddle those behind was a terrifically stupid act that I really enjoyed.

I did not understand the word responsibility until 1964 when the Club went camping in the dry bed of Pineapple Creek. This annual weekend was like running away from home and roughing it, with the safety catch on. There were two large groups of us, those from ten to fifteen and those older than that. Anyone who was older than fifteen, we thought, was so old he was already dying.

We all camped in that dry creek, talking about Donald Campbell's *Bluebird* hurtling along the salt bed of Lake Eyre at 400 miles an hour. That was fast for a boy who still rode a scooter. Our tents were strung amongst the old gums in the sand and after tea we were able to practise running in the dark and other favourite pastimes.

Running in the dark was another ritual reserved for growing boys. The older boys would belt off as a group into the hills around the camp and create an alternate site. The younger boys would know this by the flashing lights or a fire perhaps. Then it was our turn to try to find them, knowing that in the desert, on a moonless night, every sound or light could be picked up by the enemy. But not only were we smaller, we were smarter than they were, adept at creating fake travelling groups of joined torches, swift diversions and spectacular entrances.

Some nights we weren't so smart and hid up in the trees, stumbling around together in the dark, afraid to put on our lights for fear of seeing the faces we saw in our dreams. Knowing that we were making such a helpless racket that the older boys would pounce on us and we would have to run like rabbits across the desert, crying for help or falling hard in the sand near some unknown sandshoe with a bright torch beam. Holding our hearts we would get up and run again, relaxed into the cool blue, leaving the ferment of the night behind, racing off alone to lie safely in the belly of the camp creek bed.

Unlike any other time, it rained in 1964. We all fell asleep to the happy sound of drops on our canvas tents. We woke up to the rush of water around our sleeping bags. Tents were moved to the bank, clothes and boys were stacked in trees, we were saved from drowning by a fleet of kangaroo shooters in their jeeps, who ferried us over the swollen Pineapple Creek. I remember opening my eyes from an oozing sleeping bag, smelling the freshly killed meat and letting my hand glide in the rushing water as the jeep slid towards high ground.

The next weekend was even more important.

The Beatles came to Australia. Luckily it was cloudy in Broken Hill so we saw their shapes on our Pye TV. Someone in our street actually went to their concert and actually took their photo. I groaned inwardly, knowing that not all of us are chosen. All I could do was sit up late at night with the radio, going across the dial, listening to the Beatles from Brisbane, through Sydney, Melbourne and Adelaide.

Listening to the next Beatles record was always a critical moment.

What would they try to tell us this time?

It seemed like all the teenagers in the world were listening in, clamouring for directions. From 1963 to 1969, it appeared that all the keys to life were in their songs. The early songs were basic, like *Please Please Me* or *Love Me Do*, but they seemed to become more complex when we did. With *A Hard Days Night*, there was quirky comedy. When the film appeared in local cinemas, girls screamed the place down. The noise from stomping feet drowned out the sound track. Going to the movies was never so exciting.

It was the intimacy of radio that kept us with them, all the way through *Help*, *Revolver* and the intricacies of the *White Album*. It was also radio that kept us alert to the outside world, to the champions. We would listen to a test match in England, alone, late at night. Whenever there was a World Championship Heavyweight battle, it was best to listen with friends, in the warmth of a car, the radio on, relaying history through the crystals.

February 25th 1964 stands out. Cassius Clay won the Heavyweight belt when 'The Bear', Sonny Liston, failed to get up off his seat in the seventh round. 'The Invincible One' had been done! We all cheered the new champ. . .

DISCOVERING

THE BIKINI

In 1964 I bought myself a miniature camera, a Minolta. It could fit into the palm of my hand and I could see myself as the future holder of rare footage—like the Zapruder home movie of John F. Kennedy's assassination that had intrigued us all in 1963. This had been 'shot' on a home movie outfit much like my father's and formed the basis for the evidence against the assassin, as well as a host of conspiracy theories. The only problem about my Minolta was the expensive film, and my own particular belief that fingers in the frame helped prove a more genuine article.

Along with my interest in photography came a belief in fine literature. I was reading Ion Idriess and Arthur Upfield, Carter Brown and James Bond when other kids were still struggling with Enid Blyton and the comics. It was the latter two great authors who introduced me to violent action and girls. Up to that moment the closest I had got to perfect aesthetic form was watching Robin Ravelich in her blue and white striped Speedo, dive into the Broken Hill Baths on Sports Day.

It was not till Christmas 1964 that I got a closer look at perfection. During those four weeks at Durras Lakes, while I was washing the dust off along with the whiting who had been stranded in tidal pools, out of the Lake came a fifteen-year-old girl, laughing, in a bikini. She was tanned, her bikini was yellow, her hair bleached blonde. I was in love and decided to chuck out Carter Brown and turn to poetry.

I took images of my first bikini back home in 1965 but they were soon eclipsed, watching James Bond films at the local Century Theatre. This was a new theatre; the old one, according to Broken Hill tradition, being burned down by frustrated youths who couldn't go to the beach like our family. The best place for entertainment was still the Metropole on the other side of town.

Saturday afternoons at the Metropole were afternoons of grace—chips, lollies, a pasty with sauce —then there was the movie. The chance to see who was sitting next to whom, who was game enough to hold hands and risk the sweat factor. My favourite afternoon at the Metropole had nothing to do with the double feature, as it turns out. With a number of other selected warriors, I was asked to smuggle a sparrow in under my jumper. As everybody else was doing it, I was hardly going to say no, still looking like I would not survive a tussle with a bull-worker. We all slunk to our seats, nursing the quivering feathers, feeling a bit like the birds themselves in the dark. Once the movie began everyone released their sparrow and soon the whole screen was alive with squeaking birds. The management turned us all out and gave us our money back. What a great day! A week later the Metropole was burned down, but nobody blamed the birds.

In 1965 I was allowed to see *South Pacific*, as performed by the Broken Hill Repertory Company. I particularly liked the song, 'Bloody Mary', as we weren't allowed to swear in our house. I sang all the way home, to frowns:

'Bloody Mary is the . . . girl for me!'

At school we were treated to *Iolanthe* and *The Mikado*. Watching the players on stage I dreamt of repeating my performance as the lead in *The Emperor with No Clothes*, which I had made famous the year before by wearing ladies' winter underwear. However, some things weren't meant to be. Art was the lot left to me. . .

FIRST BRUSH
WITH FAME

As my grandfather, Asaph Noble Storey, was a painter, I was determined it was in the blood. I bought my first painting, a watercolour by Sidney R. Cocks, for two shillings. I studied from Walter Foster art books. I copied Indian scenes and seascapes. I went to art gallery openings. My parents hoped it was a passing phase.

At the Broken Hill Art Gallery I met Joshua Smith, the subject of William Dobell's Archibald Prize-winning portrait of 1944. He gave me a lot of time as I followed him around the gallery, clutching his signature in my autograph book. I'd spend whole afternoons watching Pro Hart oil his machine guns in his backyard at home, the guns like toys in his hands. Part of his armoury was a sort of shotgun with which he used to fire paint at terrified canvases, the effect being something like a fireworks explosion. Sometimes he'd be cleaning his more conventional paint brushes and he'd explain to me the secrets of The Geebung Polo Club, or how miners leave a two-up game. He enjoyed everything.

Pro took particular delight in showing the artworks in his back garage. "Ah Tom," Pro would purr, who did that one, just there?"

"That's a Monet, Mr Hart," I said, and it was.

"And what about this one young Tom?"

"Oh that's a Streeton Mr Hart!"

"And what about this one, near the Money?" mispronounced Pro.

"Oh that's a Hart, Mr Hart!"

Sundays were days of rest, so I often rested from going to every church service by wandering over after Sunday School to meet the artists in Sturt Park. My favourite was Sam Byrne, who was a bit like my grandfather in his work-shirt and boots. He'd sit on a chair in the sun, surrounded by little oils containing Sturt desert peas, or rabbits, raining all over a desert landscape. If you sat with him, he'd tell stories of Broken Hill when he was a boy, of tarring and feathering in the streets, miners' strikes and the great age of smelting and mining the mother lode. Most of the locals laughed at his paintings, saying they could have been done by any child. But that's what I so liked about them, the immense detail and the feeling of being there at that moment, witness to so many dramatic events in Broken Hill's past.

My art studies were hastened, I feel, by a new teacher at Broken Hill High. She was French and had more curves than a hockey stick, which made her good to study during class. I was particularly attentive that year. This was better than collecting Nude Majas as as she had no perforations and no hinges, just a French accent and pure form.

Also hiding in the folds of my autograph book were the signatures of Australian cricketers, Jarman and Favell. Both were from South Australia and they'd come up for a coaching tour. As I had found lots of cuttings of Bradman under the linoleum at our house I thought I was interested in cricket. It was years later that I learnt it was really old newspaper I was interested in. However, Barry Jarman was a jolly wicketkeeper and Les Favell was a taciturn opening bat who entertained us for a day when cricketers weren't paid, just 'made'.

Goya's Nude Maja.

HIGH SCHOOL

CONFIDENTIAL

For some reason best known to themselves, I was put in 1A by the powers that be at Broken Hill High School. At assembly I would look down the lines of eager faces from my primary grades—aisles of first year students going all the way to 1R. My best friend Peter, who had gone to 1P the year before, had repeated first year and been elevated to 1H. They don't make grades like they used to.

The first mass assembly was a startling event because of its resemblance to those American prison movies that held so many sullen faces in a walled quadrangle. While the first and second year classes were huge, by the time the kids got to fourth year there were only four tiny classes. In fifth year,

there was one alert class. They were pretty smug, knowing they were the last year of the old education system and that the rest of us kids would have to do twelve more excruciating months under the new Wyndham Scheme, if we wanted to go as far as we could. Most kids I knew didn't have that intention, however. They just wanted to leave school as soon as possible, get a job in the mines and drive an old Holden flat out on the road to the South Australian border.

Friends from primary school in lower grades grew apart from those in the top classes. It's a pity they couldn't see my report cards—I could have used the sympathy. One of the wildest, Eric, used to take imaginary rides on a motorcycle that was stranded in his back yard, rusting after his father's last terrible accident. Eric died, aged fifteen, in a crash on the road to the Pinnacles, the South Australian border only twenty miles away.

I wasn't really interested in driving, mostly because my brother was really good at it and my father could make his own cars. Their profound abilities alleviated my own responsibility in this area of manhood. Also, after I had driven my father's Humber Super Snipe around the block, being careful to park it exactly in the tyre tracks of our gravel drive, I'd got bored. Been .there, done that.

I was more concerned with trying to catch the Beatles on the radio and watching girls at swimming carnivals.

Because our school was so large, my favourite game was to create fanciful arrangements to get myself and others excused from certain harrowing periods. I was excused from English by a larrikin from third year who would come to the door and say, carefully, that the headmaster would like to see me. Shock horror. I would grimace, nervously rearrange my books and say softly, to the class: 'The horror . . . the horror. . .' Departing to nervous laughter, I would go to another class and relieve another friend. In this way we initiated the first prisoner release system in New South Wales.

This 1966 High School photograph reveals the author as a quiet,
reflective type with black skivvy and natural pompadour.

WHY I WAS NOT
IN VIETNAM

Summer evenings in Broken Hill were a time for long walks towards anything with a light on. My favourite place was Sturt Park at night when local fairs were held by some community club, and paper lanterns would entice me along the freshly mown grass to the fairgrounds where I could lose at hoopla or buy a toffee, with Billy Holiday's *The Man I Love*, straining through a tiny amplifier. Lying about in the night with that song and those whirring paper lanterns certainly made me dream.

I wanted to go away but I knew I didn't want to go to Vietnam. The Prime Minister, Mr Menzies, said that our troops were going. Even our troops who didn't want to go were going. In 1965 conscription had been introduced and nobody wanted to win the lottery any more. Especially me, even though I was only twelve. Anyway, artists didn't believe in wars, everybody knew that. 'Make love, not war' it said on the stationery my sister had given me for my birthday, for which I had only one reply: 'Right on!'

Instead of going to Vietnam my father took me to the Warri Gate, way up on the Queensland border, in a Rambler Ambassador. He had to go to see the road and thought I should see the dingo fence. When the big American car stopped swaying over two hundred miles of dirt road, I got out and was promptly sick on Queensland soil—in retrospect a most appropriate response to the local politics. Images of dingoes pawing the fence, trying to get out, would haunt me for years.

On the way back we stayed at the Tibooburra Hotel, the centre of one of the loneliest towns in the bush. Lizards and snakes slept on boulders that surrounded the town so I stayed close to the hotel, which was decorated by Russell Drysdale and had lovely crisp sheets. When it rained, gold specks ran down the main street, right past the post office. Some towns have all the luck.

Our intrepid journalist with secret spy camera
clutching Laugh-In cards.

KING MING GIVES US
DECIMAL CURRENCY

In January 1966 my brother had driven up from Sydney to see us in his red Javelin Jupiter, clutching a purple bank note for me. The bank note wasn't legal tender but a University student stunt in response to Prime Minister Menzies' proposal to institute a new currency. 'Royals' he wanted to call them, in keeping with his nationalist leanings. There was a fine purple portrait of 'King Ming the Merciless', as he was playfully dubbed by the Opposition.

Menzies retired in February 1966, amid national celebrations, and his Treasurer, the diminutive snorkeller Harold Holt, took over as Prime Minister of Australia. While a Romantic like me knew that February 14 was Valentine's Day, the Government dubbed this day Decimal Currency in 1966, and we had dollars and cents, not British royals.

How I loved the new money, which everybody thought looked like play money. Skilled in Monopoly, I eagerly collected one dollar notes while my parents sadly handed over their hard-earned pounds, shillings and pence.

After a couple of months even us children realised this was the beginning of massive inflation. When Pretty Babies leapt from four a penny to two a cent in March 1966, the Government faced a children's revolt. Threepenny ice creams were truly a thing of the past.

University students responded to the growing unrest, no doubt prompted by their younger brothers and sisters at home. When the American president, Lyndon Bains Johnson drove through the streets of our capital cities, he was jeered. Harold Holt countered with a catch phrase, so simple even liberal voters could repeat it: 'All the way with L.B.J.!' More students demonstrated and pelted both with rotten egg bombs and strong pong. 'Australia out of Vietnam!' they yelled in their blue jeans and T-shirts. I rebelled too and bought a tiny studded belt and a long floppy jumper under which to hide it.

I was almost a teenage delinquent.

A brilliant student joke - One Royal: Illegal All-leather Tender - for a good cause.

THE MYSTERIES
OF A MALVERN STAR

Everyone was preparing for the end-of-year dance when the news came. I had just demanded and received a Beatle jacket (cream with the black piping that substituted for a collar) so as to look an almost up to the minute thirteen-year-old, and was at home shining up my pointy-toe shoes on our red veranda. I was just considering who I might be game enough to dance with when Peter put his head over our stone wall.

'What you doin'?'

'Preparing to look heroic and attractive.'

'Give up! Anyway, I've got a better idea.'

'Is it as dangerous as the last one?'

I could see him thinking hard about this. Peter had suggested we form a team during the last cracker-night wars in June. We were against the two demented brothers, Gary and Marvin Shanks, alias Heckle and Jeckle. They were from North Broken Hill, were our age, and believed everything was just like in the cartoons. Including cracker-night.

Peter's brilliant idea then was a private war at his place, with unlimited hungers and fruit, as well as the creation of two 'rest' stations to hole up in. His theory was that these were safe zones. Jeckle, however, had seen too many episodes of 'The Road Runner'.

After a series of skirmishes around the almond and grapefruit trees in Peter's back yard, it was my turn to rest. Reluctantly I entered the tiny brick bunker. There was even a warm coke inside.

Squashed up in the back, looking out at the last rays of light, it was then that I saw Jeckle. He charged the bunker, cackling, in his shorts. They were loaded with bungers! There was no way out and although I pleaded safety, offered him money, anything, this was his cartoon. I bundled myself into a ball with my hands over my ears as he calmly dropped explosives into the entrance. After five minutes I was saved by one of Peter's equally distressing counter-attacks of pelted fruit. 'It's All Over Now!' he had shouted.

'The only accident you might have is falling off my bike,' Peter reassured me in the present instance.

'Where would we have to go?' I asked cautiously, clutching a shoelace.

'Just over to Railway Town Park.'

'But that's miles away. I'm not going to be dinked all that way for nothing.'

'You'll just have to miss out then ... on the girl.'

'What girl?'

The story went that tonight, in Railway Town Park, this girl from Third Form was going to rendezvous with this friend of Peter's who was in Fourth Form. Tonight. In the open. The night before the school dance.

'I'll be with you in a minute' I said.

As I still hadn't got my Malvern Star, Peter had to dink me on the bar. We talked excitedly for the first half hour, running up the hills to speed on towards the western sun. We crested the hill above Railway Town just as the sun was going down and the lights surrounding the Park were glimmering on. An aching feeling was in the pit of my stomach. I wasn't thinking about what the couple we intended spying on might 'do', but looking at the extent of the Park. It was vast and blackening quickly. Where on earth might they be? We sped down the hill to the open gates.

'Where'd he tell you he was meeting her?' I asked, faintly.

'Didn't say,' Peter replied glumly.

'Great idea' I said, reading him the number of acres the Park covered. He turned the bike round, ready to head for home.

'Reckon he wouldn't turn up anyway' he said. 'Let's go the long way home.'

BOPPING AT THE
HIGH SCHOOL HOP

Dressed to the hilt in stove-pipe black trousers, white shirt, black shoelace tie and cream Beatle jacket—and my pointy-toe shoes, I arrived at the school dance. No one recognised me. I even had to introduce myself to friends. Some of the other boys had no class.

The girls looked really glamorous, having spent all their savings on mini dresses and bouffant hairstyles, a la Dusty Springfield and Connie Stevens. If they were budding intellectuals it was long and shaggy like Jean Shrimpton and if they were truly radical, an ultra-short geometric cut, like Twiggy's. I personally thought they all looked great, especially when they rattled their bangles at me. What a night!

The band played Beatles' songs to loud applause: *Well she was just seventeen If you know what I mean…*

I had just turned thirteen, and I did.

I danced with Bronwyn Kemp because she was as silly as I was. We laughed at all the teachers prowling around making sure that we were not having too much fun. All the older boys wanted to dance with Bronwyn too so I idled by the door, looking hard done by but no one seemed to notice. The band played on. . .

They were local boys and played lots of good instrumentals that I knew like *Wild Weekend* and *Walk Don't Run*. They played the Beatles very badly, threw themselves into blacker rhythm and blues and completely failed to convince me with their version of *Doo Doo Ron Ron*. With simpler songs they fared better and when they played *Blue Moon* we all drifted round the floor. I had a habit of changing the words to songs to make them more applicable to myself and so crooned along:

Blue Moon, you saw me dancing alone

Without a girl in my arms, without a car or a phone.

I felt so deprived and so worried that they might play *A Teenager in Love* that I went home early, sauntering all the way, in my own blue heaven. One thought comforted me. Dancing in the dark very close for the first time with the smell of Imprevu, or Avon perfume bewitching the senses, and our eyes locked together, had made me feel different. It was all so easy and so delicate, the intimacy of the talk among a hundred other satellites, a mirror ball spinning gently overhead.

Three Goddesses of Broken Hill: Bronwyn,
Kim and Pam.

BOB BOTTOM

AND THE CAPSICUM

All through these school dilemmas my father worked hard at trying to join Broken Hill by bitumen road to the outside world. West to Adelaide, east to Sydney and south to Mildura. This last was his biggest problem, the road south over the ever-moving Kudji sandhills. After achieving this by what I thought was elastic road, he was interviewed by the local paper, the *Barrier Daily Truth*.

The *Truth* was a proud and efficient rag that went to every unionist. It had a good staff (one of whom was soon to be me!) which included Bob Bottom, who provided my first example of the impeccable dress sense of investigative journalists. I remember, chiefly, because it was also the day on which I discovered the capsicum.

Having been raised in a vegetable patch, grazing on shallots on the outskirts of Parkes, finding a new vegetable was a particularly unnerving moment for me. Why had my parents kept me from the joys of the capsicum, its shiny and provocative greenness, its totally addictive quality? Because up until then it hadn't been growing in our vicinity. The Italian gardener at my father's office had brought him this rare fruit. The shining pepper! I had dropped in after sport (running away from the ball) that afternoon and was sitting in the office, listening to my father talking with Bob Bottom about the art of building roads over moving sandhills, admiring them both in the vegetable glare. I carefully aligned the stalk of the 'cappo' in line with my father's nose and the other end with Bob's chin, before I ate it. A hymn of praise filled me for the Italians cultivating such a gem.

A trip to Parkes in 1965 - in search of fireballs,
or was it better television reception?

STRIKE

I had further experience of Bob Bottom in the new year of 1967 because I got a job with the *Barrier Daily Truth* as a newspaper boy. I'd wake at 4 a.m., ride into town, roll newspapers until 5 a.m. and then belt off into the dark to deliver the little bonbons. Some mornings I'd see him come in to get the paper or arrive with pen in hand, shirt out, cigarette in mouth and conspiracy theories on the brain.

Three weeks after I got the job I realised a terrible fact. Newspaper boys on the *Truth* got fifty cents less than those working for the *Barrier Miner*. Having listened so hard to Sam Byrne, my decision was inevitable—strike!

The next morning our cigar-smoking boss arrived to find us six boys playing cards instead of rolling papers. He was appalled and threw his arms about. The other boys looked at me as if to say 'Well, this was your bright idea'. Mr Ferry looked at me.

'We're not going to work till we get the same as those boys working for the *Miner* I said. 'This is a union town and we all deserve the same.' Nobody clapped. Nobody said 'Hear, hear!'. Nobody said a word. Mr Ferry gobbled on his cigar. Moments passed like days and we all sweated underneath the fluorescent lights. Then Mr Ferry turned around, took the cigar out of his mouth and said the magic word 'Okay'. A cheer went up. 'Now, get to work!' I was king for a day and received a round of milk shakes.

The best part of being a newspaper boy was delivering in the early hours, working my way through the back streets towards the Bakery. Here I'd get my choice of three freshly baked cakes for only one paper. I usually picked the biggest ones, with the most cream, and chocolate eclairs. Going into the warm white atmosphere, a fairy flour world laced with cream and chocolate after two hours of numbing cold, was heaven at the end of the line. Somehow I got home by six and woke up at eight, ready for school.

Dr Spock would have been proud.

I was tempted to spend all my money on the local races but as soon as I discovered a betting system that would always break even, it was no fun anymore. Besides, it was the end of our time in the desert. My career with newspapers was temporarily over in June and once again we locked up house and were to move to town. To the sea.

Our family had so many things—mostly because none of us kids would throw anything away. My father was a collector too, who understood us and agreed to pack all our oldest clothes, broken toys and newspaper cuttings. The only thing we left behind was our cat, who was going to live with the next people and who was perfectly happy to be staying in Broken Hill.

We left Broken Hill in June 1967 at 4 a.m., bound for Fairy Meadow. We already knew that it was not what it sounded because we'd travelled to Wollongong before. Even though we were country kids, we were smart. We knew the fairies had left long ago.

We travelled for two hours on the road to Wilcannia till just around sun-up, when my parents had a natural craving for Bushells Tea. We stopped off the main road near the only tree for miles. It was dead and so we cut some kindling for a camp fire. In the distance was the sound of roaring buffalo. By the time the water was boiling and the sun rising in the desert, an Aboriginal boundary rider had slid his old Harley Davidson to a halt, dusted down his leather and politely asked us what we were doing on the property.

Over tea and cakes he decided that we weren't going to start a bushfire. He'd seen us from five miles away and had come to investigate. Fixing us all with a big grin he pumped my hand, wishing us well. He was the last Aboriginal I'd see for a decade.

The days diminished as we came closer to civilization. The closer we got the more it looked the same. By the time we got to the sea on the top of the range of rainforest that hugs the Illawarra coastline, Broken Hill was but a haze of dust on the shimmering desert plain.

THE CINZANO KID

After the dry heat of the desert the Illawarra coast was rugged, wintry and wet. Even the sand was wet.

Wollongong High School was a selective school with a grey headmaster. Kids from all the other schools thought that our school churned out first class prigs and wimps. The most frightening thing about it though was the fact that I was a year behind in every subject.

While other boys were drawing in perspective, I was still struggling with the twelve inch rule. Girls in my art class messed with the moderns while I stuck with the primitive. In modern history, my speciality was jokes told in the trenches—to no avail. I have to admit it, I was a long way from the top of my class.

However, as always, I did have music. I could count the drum beats on any English blues track by John Mayall, could understand the chord changes of Eric Clapton and the meaning behind the Four Tops and the Supremes songs about the real degrees of Love. I was a teenager who could now sulk along with the best of them.

With my razor-sharp brain for rhythm and cadence, I knew I was a poet in the making—if only I had some experience worth writing about. I walked for miles along the beach, waiting for the muse, dreaming of purely aesthetic girl friends, with whom I could discuss Shakespeare's

Sonnets. I walked out late at night, clutching my Dr Spock, wishing I was depressed or had unhappy parents like everybody else I knew at school.

One of my closest friends was Kim, whose father ran the local paper. Mr Benjamin listened intently to my dramatic monologues about D.H. Lawrence, clutching at his own grizzly red beard. I went to parties at their place, dressed in my casual best—a double-breasted pinstripe suit jacket and black silk vest, under which resided the alcohol of teen sophisticates—Cinzano. For this scandalous behaviour I was forever dubbed the Cinzano Kid, some mothers perhaps fearing that one drop would corrupt their daughters. Or perhaps themselves.

When a friend came down from the bush one weekend in October of that year, my behaviour slipped again. Kevin was a cocky, rough-and-tumble kid who always had lived out West. It was he who found the idea of climbing Mt Keira, looking for snakes, both dangerous and attractive. Because I was the pragmatic one, he didn't quibble over my demands that we put corrugated cardboard underneath our jeans—tin men from the knees down. We bought machetes and webbed belts and simply went into the undergrowth.

The lower reaches of the mountain had walking tracks through the blackberry bushes where tiny green snakes would fire forked tongues into our strides. Did we laugh! When we found one quietly basking in the sun, we playfully chased it. As we got further up the mountain the bush had taken over. We got game and chased red-bellied black snakes, slicing off their heads. Luckily this was the last of my desert training, my stupidity.

At school things were no different. I spent all my time with 'musicians'. Warren could play trumpet to *Lonely Bull*, Gary, the drums to *Wipe Out*, Allan, the guitar to *Apache*. What a great band...

My homework suffered and school report cards from the headmaster read: 'His work appears to be fair but I am not satisfied with his attitude.' A strange coincidence. I was not satisfied with his either. The year ended with the news that our PM had drowned off Portsea in Victoria, or simply swum to China. Photographs of ASIO agents skulking along the beach haunted every newspaper. John Grey Gorton assumed the Prime Ministership. He had some flair, a larrikin touch. He'd flown Spitfires during the war which must have helped him cope with Liberal Party politics and he laughed a lot. These would be heady days.

DID THE BEATLES

HAVE DANDRUFF?

While most teenagers struggled with Clearasil and pimples, or spots as the advertising so euphemestically called them, I struggled with my hair and scalp. Every product from Silvikrin to Selsun was applied in a vain attempt to halt the snow drifts. Even when I didn't have it I thought I did and was constantly checking the shoulders of my black cardigan, disguised as enigmatic twists of the head. With a sardonic smile I would brush absent-mindedly at the problem areas, hoping to scatter the invisible enemy.

'Do the Beatles have dandruff?' I asked myself. 'Do the Stones use Selsun?' The question was akin to wondering if the Queen ever had cause to use the toilet. Of course they didn't.

While showers were for taming locks I realised that the bath brought out the meditative poet in me. Soaking in a bath for an hour or so, keeping the temperature topped up with fresh shots from the hot water system, was a good way to spend an afternoon. It put me in an idle frame of mind and took me back to the plastic toys of the past, skimming across the water of my memory.

ROCK AND ROLL

TEENAGE HEAVEN

When the Easybeats had a huge hit overseas with *Friday on My Mind* we all breathed a sigh of relief. Perhaps it was not quite so uncool to be an Australian after all. I secretly felt the Brits had only let them in because most of the group were British already. Yet there they were, dressed up in velvet suits and paisley shirts, flouncing about the Chelsea streets. Britain was thoroughly mod and of course we copied everything, with striped pants, shirts made out of the Union Jack and collars that would have looked more in place in an orthopaedic ward. The Queen had never had so many willing subjects.

Girls wore big floppy hats and sunglasses; granny glasses if they were really hip. It made them look like John Lennon. Boys would aim for sensible Australian clothing like fur coats and coloured corduroy, with handcrafted leather belts. Epaulettes were on every shoulder and those who scorned the mod look dressed tough in Amco jeans with matching cut-off jacket. The disposal stores had a field day and some youths were cool enough to wear a confederate army cap or a leather John Lennon cap, set at an insolent angle.

In Wollongong, no afternoon was complete without a visit to the Bamboo coffee lounge where you could 'catch some music'. This would inevitably be sixteen-year-old angst, played wistfully by a Bob Dylan clone and dubbed 'folk'. For the soppier among us, Donovan was the role model; for the groovers, Arlo Guthrie. Between songs we all had meaningful conversations about the state of the world or Why we were in Vietnam. I was more interested in Henry Miller and D.H. Lawrence. Neither could play guitar, sing the blues, openly take drugs or hate their parents, so I had to change my tack. Stick to music, at least in company.

I saw the Easybeats live at The Royal Easter Show. They all wore black nifty suits and white shirts so it must have been before they went to England. In the middle of one song three of them got down on their knees and Little Stevie Wright jumped over them all like a mad elf. This sent the crowd into a frenzy.

Other good bands were the Twilights and the Bee Gees, who started out by copying the Beatles. *Spicks and Specks* changed all that. More daunting were the Loved Ones, with their black rhythm and Melbourne blues. In the world of afternoon coffee lounge conversation where man's destiny seemed determined by the cappuccino intake, their urgent songs about love made them a doomed species. *Everlovin' Man*, *The Loved One* and *Sad Dark Eyes*—what a string of stark hits! Perfect for broody outsiders like myself.

On visits to Sydney I tried getting into the Cahill's restaurant. There were always musicians there and girls who looked like models and callow school children like myself, looking at the musicians and the models. It was a place where teenagers could actually get a glass of wine without having to stand on a box or produce their bus pass. Girls seemed to prefer sparkling burgundy, while boys drank claret that was rougher than any fight they'd ever found themselves in at school. It was crowded and exciting and all the women seemed so beautiful.

Gonna have fun in the city,
Be with my girl she's so pretty

I became so obsessed with Swinging London that I decided to find a British friend at school. He was older than me and came from Hampstead Heath: 'Keith, Keith from Hampstead Heath plays the Selmer saxophone with his teeth.'

I thought the Hollies could definitely do a lot with it.

We were both poets but his poetry was more musical than mine. He knew all about Swinging London and could pronounce all the Cockney words correctly. I was still having trouble with standard English.

We discussed important matters of the day, like British football results, England winning the World Cup, clean-cut Cliff Richards in *Summer Holiday*, how Hitler could have won the War, that Richard Nixon was like the Emperor Tiberius—senile! We talked about love and basketball, Beatle records and the cricket. Was Bobby Simpson losing his touch? What about that upstart Ian Chappell? He was good, but was it cricket?

As we plotted the Easybeats' next move to world domination of the record charts (by releasing *Sorry* or *She's So Fine*) we played chess stoically, just like they did in Britain.

Dr Spock, and his tricksy sign of Peace. We could read his hand.

IS THAT YOU,

DR SPOCK?

'He' was on TV. I couldn't believe it. I'd been haunted by the man, and no wonder. There, on *Star Trek*, was Mr Spock, from another planet, with blue blood, no feelings and pointy ears. What had my parents ever seen in him? Had they also been to Vulcan?

I wanted him to tell me telepathically the answers to those burning questions every teenager asked: 'Why were we in Vietnam?' and 'Was Paul McCartney *really* dead?'

'No way,' Mr Spock told me, 'Tom, being a Vulcan teenager like your-self, life will always be difficult.'

So much for good news from afar.

PEOPLE
POLITICS
AND
POP
AUSTRALIANS IN THE
SIXTIES
BY CRAIG McGREGOR
ILLUSTRATED MARTIN SHARP

AGE QUOD AGIS—1968

This quaint Latin phrase was our school motto and meant 'Pursuit of Excellence'. In assembly all our headmaster's words seemed like Latin to me.

'Join the cadets, today! Don't wear black cardigans! Get a haircut Tom! Stop talking!' Impenetrables like that.

1968 was the year that the Broadway Musical struck back with *Hair*. 1968 epitomised the struggle to keep my own. My father preferred the old- fashioned approach. Soft talking me into a straight-backed chair, then tying me up with a grey plastic raincoat.

'But Father, I wash my hair. . .' I would plead.

'Your sisters wash and iron theirs', was his irrefutable logic. Squealing for help to no avail. My mother would sometimes approach the carnage, but only to say sweetly: 'More off the sides Geoff'.

They were golden days.

In March Lord Casey arrived at our school to address the assembly. We all stood looking at the dais underneath a row of flame trees, counting the minutes. Just as the Lord arose to speak the heavens opened and we all fled for shelter, leaving our seething masters.

That summer bushfires threatened a strip of coastal towns. Every afternoon for a week I changed into my father's overalls and hitch-hiked up to the mountain to fight the fires with all the other hapless youths, miming those immortal words by Bobby and Laurie:

Like a restless tiger, you can't stand still . . .
and you never will.

We threw ourselves into our work. Sometimes till midnight we were shifted in utes all over the Broken Back Ranges, beating out spot fires, saving houses, eating pies and protecting possums. I felt so compassionate I even saved a snake, picking him up by the tail and whirling him off the fiery ridge. Somehow none of us got burnt.

More importantly, our school was visited by R.F.X. Connor, the local Member of Parliament who would later try to buy back the farm as Minister for Energy and Resources in the early 1970s. He made you think politics were worth it, that there could be dignity in labour, that mateship was important—school even. Unfortunately my June report card still read 'C for conduct is disturbing'. Our school didn't have a 'D'.

School boys front up for the October 1968 bushfires on the Illawarra
escarpment.

TEENAGE BLUES

The radio told me that the beach was the place to go for fun, fun, fun. It's what everybody had. There was no mention of sunburn, skin cancer, sandflies or sharks. There were girls on every speck of sand, boys riding every wave and Ward 'Pally' Austin on every transistor.

Ward Baby was the D.J. favoured by the beach P.A. system. He obviously had friends in high places. Ward would speak of chicks and guys, and candy-apple-red Ford Mustangs, and sign off with a 'Rickapoodly and a Fandoodly'. Along with 2UE's Mad Mell he was our answer to America's Wolfman Jack. For older people there was always Bob Rogers.

From the surf sheds on North Wollongong Beach, things looked grim to me. Everybody had a tan except me. I didn't even have a cozzie line. Not only was I skinny, white and sensitive, but I couldn't surf. Clearly the beach was no place for poets. I had one saving grace though. I could talk to girls and get meaningful about music.

Other boys from school kicked sand in my face.

'Thanks, I like sand' I would reply ironically. They'd shake their heads and go off surfing with their mates, leaving me with the girls, which was just the way I wanted it.

I wondered if California girls were like the ones I knew in Wollongong. Did they peroxide their hair for instance, and have a Coppertone tan?

Did they only talk to boys in board shorts and treat all boys in the more figure-hugging Speedos as 'dags'? Did they always have a new bikini and beach towel every season? Did they wear those curious tubes of clothing known as shifts? Indian sandals? Shorts? Could California girls always face the beach?

Not that our Austral girls went into the surf much. It was way too rough on the hair and the thickly applied coats of mascara. They waited in groups for guys, preferably glistening with salty water and carrying a surfboard nonchalantly under one arm, who might walk back to the bus with them or buy them hot chips. They wore good sunglasses and carried little cane baskets full of combs and cosmetics.

If you didn't like the beach in summer—tough luck. Perhaps I should have started that Charles Atlas course after all. . .

With the bushfires over and the beach a no-win situation, I had to find an outlet for all my excess energy. I was too young to drive so I took up long-distance running. Our school sports master 'Basher' Downs was delighted, as Wollongong High had a good reputation in cross-country events. I found his training sessions disturbing. Basher would stalk around on the spot in a red tracksuit (he was years before his time fashion-wise), his bald head shining like a beacon at the other end of the oval, yelling at anybody in sight. Even if you were running really fast. Some of the kids had been trained from the cradle by Basher and would really belt along. I liked running but sweating profusely was another matter.

The results of my first big competition: 'David Novy, Ian McDonald, John Capper and Tom Thompson left nothing in doubt as to their slashing team's victory in the Under-15, 1 and half mile event.' Graciously I accepted my medal.

In the Olympics, Australian Ric Mitchell ran second for a silver medal in the 440 yards. Basher was jubilant.

As Basher would say – 'Boys – and you too Thompson!' (as if I was another entity), watch Ric Mitchell glide into that corner, arms not too high, he is an engine now, moving into the straight; slightly extending his gait now, getting past his defence. Look at his eyes, wheeling now for home. Going for the Gold now...'

'He's going for Silver, Sir!'

'Shut up Thompson! He's throwing everything he can at it – that's what I want from you boys. A marathon mentality!'

Basher was right.

All that running made me strong enough for late-night marathon dancing at the dingy, black with fluorescent paint cave in Kenny Street called a disco, Zondrae's. It was owned by Zondrae King who gamely allowed my friends to play under a number of pseudonyms to ever-diminishing audiences. I often played bass, at least I played some of the strings—but not being allowed out during the week, my days as a rock superstar were numbered.

Because fifteen-year-old boys were all sensitive and unhappy, I formed a local chapter of the Australian Blues Society. I knew 'down home' singers like Blind Willie McTell and Robert Johnson intimately and every Bessie Smith track. I oozed confidence among record catalogues and transcriptions of twelve-string recordings. I even wrote my own blues:

The Teenage Blues
My baby left me for another guy,
I'm a dag, I don't know the reason why.
The nights are cold, my car's out of gas—
If I only had one, I'd get away real fast,
And I'm too young to booze. . .
I got the teenage blues. . .
(guitar solo followed by restless sighs).

Aged 15 I was ready to part my hair in the middle and grow it really long (if only). My mother had other, more genteel ideas...

TELEVISION

Still, staying at home at night wasn't so bad. There was television. *Bell-bird* at six o'clock, *Commotion* to follow, *You Can't See Round Corners* and *Homicide* at night. After Robert Kennedy and Martin Luther King were assassinated the public demanded more comedy to blot out the reality, so it was more *Dick Van Dyke*, more *F-Troop*, more *Flying Nun*.

We watched TV while we ate dinner every night. Chops and chips and vegetables, hopefully before the News. If we were still eating dessert and something awful happened on the ABC News, it really soured the evening. My father would have us turn down the sound and we'd eat our ice cream and jelly in silence.

Television had gone inter-global. We watched the Olympic Games from Mexico, and Aboriginal boxer, Lionel Rose, beat Fighting Harada in Japan for the World Bantamweight Title. More importantly I was now old enough to see *The Saint*, *The Man from U.N.C.L.E.* and *The Avengers*, with Mr Steed and Mrs Emma Peel. Raucous laughter from Alf Garnett in *Till Death Us Do Part*, or hip humour from Rowan and Martin's *Laugh In*, helped to keep the Vulcan blues away.

I began writing 'seriously' for poetry magazines, prizes and newspapers, usually under pseudonyms like Ezekial Smith or Kent Goddard. Some of the magazines held advertisements of swirling hippies in rooms full of incense, or copies of overseas record covers. I stuck to my task as a poet-in-the-making and wrote poems for the cheap roneoed *Free Poetry*, a magazine edited by the grand Nigel Roberts and the upper-crust *Poetry Australia*, but everything was rejected.

I didn't live in Balmain, go game-fishing, didn't drive fast cars. Didn't drive at all. So I became political, writing *Woomera – the Musical*, on the attempted clean-up of the British nuclear test-site at Maralinga.

> *I left my heart, in Maralinga.*
> *I left my head, parts of my body too.*
> *If you get back, to Maralinga,*
> *You'll find bits of me there*
> *Waiting just for you…*

DEEP AND MEANINGFUL

CONVERSATIONS

In October 1968 I packed up my clothes and records to stay at a friend's place over the weekend. This was to be a record party. The only houses that allowed record parties, with their accompanying all-night dancing and listening, were those run by divorced mothers who wanted to dance with their school-age daughters, or talk about love to their daughters' boyfriends. Luckily I knew lots. The Age of Aquarius was taking its toll on human relationships.

Saturday afternoon in some mother's lounge room, decorated by her daughter's girlfriends with psychedelic posters, littered with music magazines and reeking of joss stick. We'd all sit around dressed up to the hilt. The girls in satins from Sydney shops like The Daily Planet or Gasworks, the boys sporting a new wide tie, or jacket culled from a lonely Indian carpet. Shoes from Mr John.

Health wasn't jogging but sunflower seeds.

'Anyone like some more seeds?' says Kim.

If we were lucky they'd be pumpkin. Coffee, some cheap flagon wine, olives, health cakes! Under an improvised strobe light, the dancing would begin to the latest records.

During the day the dancing was a free-form movement of arms and legs in the air, dancing with the head and fingers, with everyone in the

The last issue of Oz *magazine in Australia, number 41, February 1969, as drawn by Martin Sharp. Biting satire. A stylish shocker for any student.*

room. Cosmic. At night, as tiredness took over, close dancing was acceptable, hanging over your partner's shoulders like the marathon dancers in *They Shoot Horses Don't They*.

Close dancing was also permitted if the song was sensitive, deep and meaningful.

'Oh yeah, beautiful, this is my song. . .' someone would say, dropping into the partner's arms and rocking like a baby to anything from the Beatles' *White Album* or the Young Rascals' *I Ain't Gonna Eat Out My Heart Any More*. Instead of talking, the song did it for us. It was even possible to have a group conversation, ten kids in a room, drawing on our cigarettes listening to the Cream's *White Room*, all relating: '*In a white room, with black curtains, is a station. . .*

This would remind one of a dream they'd had, another of their own room before their parents dropped in, another of a poster drawn in San Francisco, or perhaps the major arcana of the Tarot. Poetry was accepted as often more appropriate than talk. Poetry was rarefied. Ideas in perfect form! The poetry of Kahlil Gibran was particularly enlightened and Gibran's *The Prophet* was a perfect gift to any loved one. The best poetry was the one you rolled yourself.

'Don't put on Led Zeppelin, unless it's "Stairway to Heaven" okay?'

'It's cool.'

'Led Zeppelin are a real drag, you know. Really heavy, compared to Crosby, Stills & Nash. Have you got *Dejavu*?'

'No, but I used to have it.'

'I reckon Johnnie Farnham is a real dag. I mean, *Sadie, the Cleaning Lady*? I mean really, what does it mean? It doesn't mean anything at all.'

'Right on.'

'Yeah, he's a real drag.'

'Hey, have you got *Kind of a Drag* by the Buckinghams?'

'You mean, "*Kind of a drag when my baby says goodbye*"?'

'Yeah, that's it, it's gas.'

'No.'

Everybody tested each other with the words of the latest hit and dreamt of the day they could 'drop out'.

Some songs just went on and on. Eric Burdon's *House of the Rising Sun* was still used by lots of bands to close off school concerts or shows because they knew everybody would get close and listen to each other's heartbeats. We could also relate to *When I was Young* because after all, we still were.

'Hey, has anybody got any pot?' The call of the local drug fiend, a late arrival. Long John would wander in still wearing his sunglasses, caught between two stereotypes: the hippie and the beatnik. He never dressed up for parties, he dressed down, but down in the finest torn and dirty blue jeans and Indian shirt. He usually dropped out of the conversation after ten minutes of frenzied dancing to the Who's *I'm A Boy*.

'*I'm a boy, I'm a boy but my ma won't admit it...*'

Was he trying to tell us something?

'You're already stoned man. Sit down and have some herbal tea.'

'You call this out of it?' John would squeal, falling to his knees in a pile.

'Anybody got any heads?'

'John, when are you going to grow up?' says Wendy, applying kajal to her eyelids.

'Blow up? Me?'

'Yes John, have a Metro Gum.'

Even if most of us weren't on drugs, there was still a lot of giggling.

MEETING THE
MAGIC PUDDING

In the late sixties I went up to Sydney on the train on Saturday mornings to scrounge through Ashwoods in Pitt Street for books and records. To bring back another Penguin classic would satisfy me for at least another week.

I haunted the arcades of Sydney between George and Castlereagh Streets, looking at rare and ancient stamps so I wouldn't have to buy them, camera and clothing stores and the inevitable book shops. Angus & Robertson in Castlereagh Street was the best. Not only did it have quality books direct from the sunny U.K. but it had a bookseller, Mr Hedley Jeffries. He always dressed well, snappily conservative! How he could talk. Sometimes I stayed an hour or two just to listen to him. And every time he'd talk, he'd sell books. It was wonderful.

One Saturday afternoon Hedley introduced me to Norman Lindsay, who was signing some copies of the Jubilee edition of *The Magic Pudding*. Norman was fragile and white but there was still a lot of power in the knuckles of his right hand. He asked me if I liked *The Magic Pudding*, to which I replied:

'Mr Lindsay, I was reared on your Pudding.'

This seemed to cheer him up a great deal. I was impressed by the fact that he obviously had never bothered to take a Charles Atlas course either. I could not afford to buy the Jubilee edition of *The Magic Pudding*. Anyway, I already had a really old copy from my grandmother, and I wasn't going to let slip how I was also reared on May Gibbs' Gumnut Babies. Sometimes you've just got to hold back the truth. I was invited back to Hedley's 'room', a cupboard under the stairwell, Hedley taking Norman by the arm, off into the world of books. I was hooked.

Sydney was the home of 'the cool people', the sensitive romantics. From the outside it seemed everybody in Sydney indulged in free love, went to discos until 3 a.m. 'dropped' acid, smoked pot and listened to Jimi Hendrix and Janis Joplin. Bands like Heart and Soul delivered a black brassy version of American funk under strobe lights and colour wheels. If you were really lucky you might get a full light show, with optional fog to dance in. Bands like Tully seemed permanently shrouded in fog but then that was part of their magic.

Getting up to Sydney was the biggest event of the week and gave the biggest 'high'. I usually took the train, but having so little money, I used to get a lift with someone older and wealthier, whenever possible.

If I was driven up by one of the Rink brothers I'd have to hold on tight. Ed Rink had a blue FJ Holden. He'd spent more money on the sound system than the safety requirements and a carload of boys, going to Sydney, was always close to hysteria. When he stopped at traffic lights he'd make us all get out of the car and dance around it till the lights changed. Music blared from the windows —'Like a Whole-lotta-love!'—and we dropped back exhausted into our seats, laughing uproariously, 'letting it all hang out'. Luckily we never had an accident and we never saw 'the fuzz'.

The tension of those trips however, cured me from driving for life.

HAIR

In 1969 I bought a pair of knee-length Spanish riding boots to go with my pin-stripe jacket and black hat. My mother thought I looked ridiculous. I thought I looked almost inhumanly suave.

By now my interest in rock-and-roll had at last paid off when I was allowed to write the Wollongong column in the national music weekly, *Go Set*. I again used a number of pseudonyms and particularly enjoyed the feeling of getting into the Wonderland Ballroom to review the Beach Boys— for nothing! The Ballroom was an old tenpin bowling alley that had bit the dust for culture. When groups like Tully played, there'd be light shows by Ellis D. Fogg. Everybody freaked out in the fog, dancing in a frenzy of whirling limbs, arms held high up in the air pretending they were Indian love gods. One friend of mine was busily selling off pounds of tarragon, a natural herb that smelt just like pot, by the matchbox-load. Soon the dupes were 'getting high' on tarragon and the price of the herb soared at the local Natural Food Centre—from 40 cents to $2 per pound. With such high overheads my friend cut out while the going was good.

Another wild drug was my own invention. Peter Stuyvesants smeared with Macleans Toothpaste. 'All over the world. . .Paris, Rome, Wollongong. . .' A group of us would enter a disco and coolly light up a smeared

Tom with guitarist Allan vander Linden, "studying" for exams in November 1969, as photographed by the Illawarra Mercury. *Our headmaster was not amused. 'Long hair on boys was completely unnecessary,' he said. 'I cannot adjust to the appearance of some of my students.'*

Stuyvo. Again, the smell was exactly like high-grade dope. Soon there were a few longhaired bikers in their denims, sniffing around us, giggling:

'Hey man, what's that you're smokin'?'

I'd look up dreamily, then catch an eye—'Toothpaste.'

'Oh wow, toothpaste eh. Can we have some of your toothpaste!'

Ah, I was generous then. . .

After six months I lost my job with *Go Set*. There was something wrong with the copy they said—too many jokes.

'This is an information column, not a funny page.'

I sulked for days. However, I still used my card to see Doug Parkinson in Focus and *Big Time Operator* Jeff St. John.

When the Masters Apprentices tried to strut their stuff at David Jones Department Store on Saturday morning, I realised that things were changing, the music was not so glamorous. Perhaps it was too early in the day for rock musicians? It was like having a hangover. They looked terrible, sang off-key and somehow shuffled along. Girls crooned. Boys wept. Old men grumbled at their long hair and their glam-rock suits. I decided that their records would still do me though: 'Living in a child's dream. . .'

Local opposition to conscripting our boys for Vietnam was hotting up. The war zone seemed to b extending all the way to Wollongong. When HMAS Melbourne collided with the US destroyer Frank E. Evans in the South China Sea, seventy-four men were killed. This event seemed to underline the stupidity of it all. Both ships were fighting for the same side.

Mac Gudgeon lived down the road in a very normal household. He was called up, didn't want to go and went AWOL instead. He talked with unionists on the south coast who gave him great support. The federal police would chase him from place to place only to find in the papers the next day that Mac had been talking to railway workers or journalists in a completely different spot. We spent many nights together walking down by the harbour, talking of blues music and poetry and films like *Easy Rider*, where freedom was the beginning and the end. Mac was never caught, worked in a health- food restaurant and later wrote a series for TV, *Waterfront*.

Television in 1969 had dropped comedy again for the heroic jaw of Gerard Kennedy in *Division 4*, where local cops licked crims. Lionel Rose beat Alan Rudkin to retain the Bantamweight crown and the ABC went mad and gave teenagers their own weekly program, *GTK*, with the debonair Chris Winter. Film clips of overseas groups like Vanilla Fudge, overhauling the Beatles' classic *Eleanor Rigby*, were a weekly treat.

In 1969 the musical *Hair* was finally playing up in Sydney and everybody was growing their own. Coloured scarves were allowed around the hair itself, inevitably becoming the American Indian version of the headband, to keep the savage locks held back from important activities like playing the guitar or operating a band-saw at work. Having been guided by a classical upbringing I tried to write a poem for the *Sydney Morning Herald*, whose pages were beset with gum leaves and bush tales. Way ahead of its time, it was rejected:

When I Brush my Hair
Hair, is a wonderful arrangement
Just like an orchestra . . .
If Gustav Mahler can do it in five parts
Why can't I?
Hair, is such a wonderful attraction—
Everyone wants to have it (but only on the head).
Who cares about the moulting process
Why, not me!

Going to see *Hair* live on stage in Sydney was the event of the year. At the end of Act One, the whole cast appeared naked to sing something about the Age of Aquarius. As most of the audience, at least those from Wollongong, still hadn't seen members of the opposite sex nude, this proved to be a great drawcard. Some were so shocked they did not venture back in after the interval, but retired to a Kings Cross coffee bar to work it through.

While nudity was 'beautiful' clothes were 'where it's at'. Clothes shops modelled on London's Carnaby Street appeared in Sydney. The Daily Planet operated in Her Majesty's Arcade, Merivale's in Castlereagh Street and Mr John's in King Street. There were a staggering number of very tall, very beautiful women working in the Merivale shop who seemed straight out of the London magazines with their ultra-modish clothes and heavy Mary Quant make up. There was Gasworks in Rowe Street for girls and

The Inn Shoppe in Hunter Street for fashion-conscious boys. Shirts and wide, wide ties were all the rage and The Inn Shoppe seemed to have an inexhaustible supply of big collars.

But it was Winter in Wollongong not Summer in the City. We had our own fabulous plan. As we didn't have a car, we were bold and went where most men feared to tread – Dwyers Car Yard, late at night. I discovered that they had an ancient black hearse there for sale, with a radio and they didn't lock it up at night. Thus Wendy, Kim and I could have our own party, with our own music, in our own car, late at night, at no cost. Under the moon, the chrome and duco of fabulous Fords and hunkering Holdens, gripped me in the passenger seat, and I thought I'd buy the hearse, just for the radio.

John Ruffels was a charismatic speaker at Sydney's Domain.
Even I could relate to the Young, Social *and* Now *rhetoric.*

1969 in Sydney's Domain. Photograph by John Ruffels.

MOONDANCE

On July 20 1969 we were all herded into the school gym to watch the first men on the moon. As it was live, we were all looking forward to any slip-ups— undone shoelaces, unconscious use of expletives, that sort of thing. Being so tall I was twenty rows from the front, struggling to ascertain what was going on. The TV was black-and-white, a twenty-two inch set. Amongst the shadows, snow and ice of the moon, we all admired a bumbling white blow-up suit—Neil Armstrong—who made the first footprint on the lunar surface. Then feeling the weight of the world on his shoulders, he said:

One small step for man, one giant step for mankind.

I had a feeling of dejavu as I watched the lunar surface. It all looked so familiar and then I realised it was a throwback to my close encounters with sea sponges, in the privacy of my own bathroom.

In the deep and lulling silence, I found myself going deeper, way back to the very beginning in Parkes. The moon landing was being relayed to our television screens by the Parkes Radio Telescope, and pretty soon I felt a fireball coming through our gym at belly-height.

'Hold everything,' I said, strangely getting everybody's attention.

Four hundred faces moved from the tiny screen to peer at me.

Basher Downs was looking at me sternly.

'Sir! Mr Armstrong is winding up now, quite relaxed but he's moving faster now. He's going for Gold!'

Everybody locked in to the tiny screen.

'Wait!' I said, and an audible in-breath sucked up the gym. 'He's running sir, he's running on the moon!'

I looked eagerly at the television for a banana peel.

Then out came Ed Aldrin. Poor Ed, relegated in history to the second man on the moon. We watched them both bound about and plant the flag. They probably cried and sang *God Bless America*. And that was it. The end to all those romantic songs like *Blue Moon*. They all fell into a heap of dust at Ed Aldrin's feet.

Australia applauded. T. V. Week, with its finger on the public pulse, gave the astronauts a Special Gold Logie for their appearance on our screens that year. Although almost everybody watched Prince Charles get invested as the Prince of Wales, Charles didn't get any award at all. Not even an ordinary Gold Logie. As teenagers we'd stopped thinking James Bond movies were the ultimate and had progressed to Modesty Blaise and Blow Up. Op art and pop art, pop music and pop films.

With memories of all that moon-dancing the film we all related to that year was *2001: A Space Odyssey*, especially as nobody could understand the ending. Nearly three hours of classical German music and American space technology, all steeped in mysticism. HEAVY!

*Drummer Gary Norwell and band live at
Centennial Park. Tom is hiding behind the
cymbal, like most poets do.*

MAKE LOVE
NOT WAR

The Fifth Formers in our school were producing another newspaper, called *First Edition*. It cost 5 cents and included serious articles like 'Why I support the Vietnam Moratorium' and more importantly, film and record reviews by Peter Christmas (another useful pseudonym). A head of my time, I reviewed *Easy Rider* and *Butch Cassidy and the Sundance Kid* positively!

I made my last stage appearance of the sixties at our annual Market Day, along with other members of the King Biscuit Band. We came on twenty minutes late, the compere telling students that I'd been taking the curlers out of my hair. During the third song I realised the microphone was faulty but this had the effect of enhancing the band's performance. We were even written up in the school magazine by a grudging admirer: 'Last on the programme was The King Biscuit Band who made you listen because you could not hear anything else.'

The headmaster seemed to agree in my end-of-year report.

'Once again C for conduct tells most of the story. It's time he matured.'

I think my mother cried and I thought about running away from home.

Well, running anyway. I had kept up my training and done alright in the regional cross-country runs, so much was expected of me for the premier race on Sports Day—the mile. Basher Downs was in a green tracksuit, waiting for us all at the end of the course, slapping a ruler against his trouser leg. I was determined to run fast, even if I wasn't running away from home and belted out in front to the groans of the others.

About half-way round the circuit it started to rain. The rain fell on my hair and suddenly I was overtaken by Aquarian rebellion and irresponsibility. I began dancing on the spot like I heard they had done at the Woodstock Pop Festival. I waited for all the other runners to catch up with me, chanting 'No rain, no rain!' but they declined to join me and instead flew past in a fever of Right- wing competitiveness. Damn!

Basher Downs was screaming, I knew not what. I got back into the race and was soon in third place, nearing Basher, slapping his ruler, clearly furious. I careered off the running track and raced for my clothes near the bike sheds with his voice shrill in my ears:

'Thompson! I'll kill him!'

All in all discipline had become quite a problem at the school. What with student interest in the anti- conscription campaign and *The Little Bed School Book* talking of student rights (not to mention private parts) and teachers openly reading *Teaching As A Subversive Activity*, our school was on the skids. There was much concern and breast-beating over the declining strength of the School Cadet Unit.

'Why did only 27 boys attend camp this year when a few years ago over 75 attended?' asked a Corporal in the school magazine.

'Because we want to make love, not war, man' was the unspoken editorial comment.

The year ended in an expectant mood, not just for the new year or the new decade but the fact that we were going to have a new headmaster. In February 1970, the era of T.K. Gardiner began, bringing with it fun, tolerance and diversity, on which we all thrived. Students became part of the decision-making process and many oddballs found a home at last.

Yes, the Sixties were an innocent zone where teenagers longed to dress up, had high ideals and did silly things. Where the dream of being a public person, a success, seemed far away and not such a necessary place to visit. The idea of individual freedom was paramount, from Dr Spock through to John Lennon, even if it did cave in a bit in 1969 with the Beatles breaking up and the drug related deaths of Jimi Hendrix and Janis Joplin.

With Elizabeth Denley at a Jumping Sunday, Centennial Park. A violin was de rigueur in those days. Photograph by Ted Harvey.

Teenagers had become politicised. Seeing older friends attacked in demonstrations the magic television-consciousness revealing every secret. Decisions were polarised. Should I be a poet or a cadet? The answer was so simple. Everybody was creative. Everybody was 'an artist'. In January the following year I helped to organise a music festival in the Southern Highlands, Fairlight; four miles south of Mittagong. 'Bring girls, beads, bright banners and things to share. Wear your happiness in colours and leave your watches at home!' With school friends we had a fruit stall with the sign STONED FRUIT. Police loitered around the tent expecting drug deals with the peaches, but alas, no luck.

Everything had changed. You could actually debate the virtues of a possible Labor Government. You could actually conceive of a possible Labor Government. It was possible to talk in assembly. I started a film club with a 50 cent membership just to see Jane Fonda in *Barefoot in the Park* and Jean-Luc Godard's *Breathless*.

In 1964 Cassius Clay had become Heavyweight Champion of the World and now changed his name to Muhammad Ali—from 'slave' to Black Muslim. Every Right-thinking American made him pay for it in 1967 with a complete suspension for refusing military service. He kept his religious beliefs and came back to fight Joe Frazier in 1970.

In 1970 there was *Woodstock*—'Three days of Love and Peace'—on film. This spawned a number of local versions, at Nimbin, Fairlight, Ourimbah and Sunbury. The film *Women in Love* brought D.H. Lawrence to the screen, with its deep and meaningful discussion of the com-plexities of 'free love'. Typical party fare would be a teenage recreation of Alan Bates as Lawrence's hero, seriously splitting a fig.

Throughout the sixties the religions and mystical values of the East were discussed as alternatives, much to the chagrin of local church leaders. Teenagers ventured into the occult, the world of astrology, palmistry and the Tarot. The work ethic was not the first ethic one was thinking about after leaving school.

Creativity was something personal and real, something fluid and worth demonstrating.

We all oozed confidence.

Next stop, the Seventies...

An audio edition of this book, complete with music by King Biscuit and Dog Trumpet, is available from Bolinda Audio.

Printed in Australia
AUHW012024230120
322831AU00004B/12

9 780648 739029